MANAGING GLOBALLY

S0-AXI-885

TERENCE BRAKE

LONDON, NEW YORK, MUNICH,
MELBOURNE, AND DELHI

Senior Editors Amy Corzine
and Jacky Jackson
Senior Art Editor Sarah Cowley
DTP Designers Julian Dams
Production Manager Michelle Thomas
US Editors Gary Werner and
Margaret Parrish

Managing Editor Adèle Hayward
Managing Art Editor Karen Self

Produced for Dorling Kindersley by

13 SOUTHGATE STREET WINCHESTER HAMPSHIRE SO23 9DZ

Editors Kate Hayward, Jo Weeks
Designers Laura Watson, Elaine C Monaghan

First American Edition, 2002
02 03 04 05 10 9 8 7 6 5 4 3 2 1

Published in the United States by
Dorling Kindersley Publishing, Inc.
95 Madison Avenue, New York, New York 10016

Copyright © 2002 Dorling Kindersley Limited
Text copyright © 2002 Terence Brake

All rights reserved under International and Pan-American
Copyright Conventions. No part of this publication may
be reproduced, stored in a retrieval system, or transmitted
in any form or by any means, electronic, mechanical,
photocopying, recording, or otherwise, without the prior
written permission of the copyright owner. Published in
Great Britain by Dorling Kindersley Limited.

Library of Congress Cataloging-in-Publication Data

Brake, Terence.–
Managing globally / Terence Brake. -- 1st American ed.
p. cm.-- (Essential managers)
Includes index.
ISBN 0-7894-8413-7 (alk. paper)
1. International business enterprises--Management.
2. Globalization--Economic aspects. 3. Competition,
International. I. Title. II. Series.

HD62.4 .B72 2002
658'.049--dc21   2001047628

Reproduced by Colourscan, Singapore
Printed and bound in Hong Kong by Wing King Tong

See our complete product line at
www.dk.com

CONTENTS

WORKING PRACTICES

LEADING GLOBAL TEAMS

INTRODUCTION

*O*rganizations *from every part of the world are reaching out beyond their domestic markets to become international players. Not only is this very demanding on the businesses themselves, but it also creates a challenge for individual managers who must cope with working across geographic and cultural borders. Managing Globally teaches you how to succeed in this new world. It provides clear systems and approaches to help you manage global networks and teams, and it examines the skills needed for dealing with different cultures. Practical advice, including 101 concise tips, helps you to achieve the best results for you and your team. Finally, a self-assessment exercise enables you to evaluate your global management skills.*

SUCCEEDING AS A GLOBAL MANAGER

For an organization to succeed on a global scale, a radical shift in business procedures is required. To become a successful global manager, aim to develop a global outlook.

WHAT IS GLOBALIZATION?

There are many definitions of the term "globalization." Develop an understanding of what it is in terms of business and why it is important to your organization in particular. Be ready to deal with the challenge of global complexity.

1 Become the best informed person on globalization that you know.

▲ **SHRINKING THE WORLD**
One of the most rewarding aspects of being a global manager is the chance to make close business relationships with people from all over the world.

DEFINING GLOBALIZATION

In business, globalization is the trend toward an integrated worldwide economy. It is seen increasingly in markets, finance, production, and logistics. Politics has created global opportunities, economics has provided the incentives, and technology the means. In a broader sense, globalization is a process in which local lives are increasingly influenced by global forces, leading to greater cultural interaction.

2 Use all the technologies available to you so that you can communicate globally.

COOPERATING GLOBALLY

Globalization has evolved slowly. In the twentieth century, new institutions for economic cooperation between advanced industrial nations were formed as a result of the two devastating world wars. These included the World Bank, International Monetary Fund (IMF), and General Agreement on Tariffs and Trade (GATT). Later, the fall of the Berlin Wall (1989) and the collapse of the Soviet Union (1992) triggered increased democratization, along with deregulation of markets.

LOOKING AT MARKETS

New and emerging markets provide opportunities for businesses to improve their revenues. While every country has its own unique culture, many new and emerging markets have growing middle classes who are willing and able to spend money on global brands. Think about how your organization could enter new markets and reduce costs, for example, by increasing the scale of the production or by shifting it to a cheaper cost location.

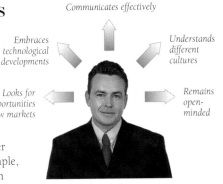

Communicates effectively

Embraces technological developments

Understands different cultures

Looks for opportunities in new markets

Remains open-minded

THINKING GLOBALLY

3 Keep up to date with new technologies.

4 Be prepared for sudden and rapid changes.

ADOPTING NEW TECHNOLOGIES

Ongoing developments in transportation and communication are dramatically increasing the flow of people, goods, capital, information, and ideas across borders. Previous constraints of time and space have dissolved in a world shaped by the internet, intranets, satellite television, and mobile telecommunications. Understand how a new technological infrastructure can redefine your notions of what business can be done, and from where, when, and how.

UNDERSTANDING THE GLOBALIZATION PROCESS

A global manager needs to know what point his or her organization has reached in the globalization process, and where it wants to go. Understand the process and recognize the strategies that will give your organization a global advantage.

5 Find out about your organization's plans for global development.

POINTS TO REMEMBER

- Having subsidiaries worldwide is not the same as operating as a single global organization.
- Even a small, domestic business can become a global organization.
- Adapting to global markets requires a great amount of personal and organizational learning.

OPERATING NATIONALLY

A national or domestic business is based solely in its home market. Such a firm has not made any Foreign Direct Investment (FDI) to set up international operations. However, it can enter the international marketplace by licensing its products and services, by franchising, or by exporting. Be aware that in free-trade economies, a domestic business is always in danger of losing its home market to more competitive global firms.

OPERATING INTERNATIONALLY

When a domestic organization's international activities reach a certain size, it will probably establish an international division to monitor cross-border transactions, such as the licensing of rights, the setting up of franchise operations, or the exporting of products. Then, a sales office may be opened in another country, or a joint venture partnership established with a foreign business. Consider how partnering can help you gain access to new markets – it can significantly reduce the amount of research you need to do in order to succeed in a new territory.

6 Identify your organization's global potential.

7 Make sure that your management team shares a global vision.

CREATING A MULTINATIONAL

As an international business expands, it develops a physical presence (subsidiaries) in multiple countries. It might do this through mergers and acquisitions or by creating new operations. Power tends to be distributed geographically, with each country unit focused on doing business and performing a range of functions, including sales and customer service, in its own territory. The challenge is to coordinate product development and manage brands across geographical borders.

8 Identify how your organization intends to reach its global targets and what obstacles are in its way.

▲ **BEING PREPARED**
Before an overseas business meeting, take some time to refresh everyone's minds on the main goals of the trip, so that your team is focused before the meeting.

EVOLVING INTO A GLOBAL ORGANIZATION

The next challenge is to integrate the subsidiaries into a fully functional network: a global organization must think and act as one business worldwide, while also maintaining local responsiveness. At this stage, power usually shifts from country units to worldwide business groups, responsible for global product and brand strategies, research, and development. Recognize that excellent cross-border coordination is a critical business advantage, that will give your organization capabilities that competitors cannot easily match.

QUESTIONS TO ASK YOURSELF

Q Where can I find up-to-date information on my organization's global strategy?

Q How can I help my staff and myself to develop a global mind-set?

Q What can I do in my area to support global coordination of the business?

Q Are our operating methods in line with best practices from around the world?

IDENTIFYING GLOBAL BUSINESS CAPABILITIES

Every global manager needs to develop the vision necessary to succeed in the integrated world economy. Understand your market, develop a clear focus, refine business processes, form a talented team, and aim to conserve your organization's identity.

9 Challenge all your existing assumptions about doing business.

QUESTIONS TO ASK YOURSELF

Q Am I keeping up to date with changing customer needs and wants worldwide?

Q Do I look for the global potential in local innovations?

Q Am I recruiting people who can handle the complexities of global business?

Q Am I rewarding my staff for identifying local and global risks and opportunities?

CUSTOMER RELATIONS ▶
As your organization achieves success in global markets, the balance of its customer base is likely to change. Local and regional customers may have less impact on your business than global ones.

10 Look for niche-market opportunities.

SCANNING THE MARKET

Monitor the global business environment to identify any opportunities and risks that could affect your organization. You should be particularly aware of industry trends, changes in your customer preferences, competitor moves in products and pricing, new technologies, legal and regulatory changes, relevant government policy changes, new methods for marketing and distribution, and new supply sources. Gather information so that you can ensure that strategic and tactical policies are based on fact, not speculation.

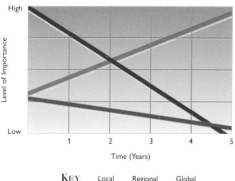

KEY   Local   Regional   Global

11 Compare your organization with its competitors.

12 Examine every aspect of your business.

DEVELOPING A FOCUS

In formulating global strategic goals, a business must have certain information. Make sure that you know who and where your customers are and how they are changing. Look at your products and services to consider which have the best potential to succeed, while requiring the least adaptation. Study strategic markets to see how they can be entered into or expanded. Finally, look at the strategies of global and local competitors: think about how they could be bettered and beaten.

LEARNING FOR COMPETITIVE ADVANTAGE

To improve its strategies, and to be able to develop and sustain its sources of competitive advantage, a business must be in a continuous state of learning. Recognize that global competitive advantage comes from at least three sources: 1) technical excellence – an ability to create, absorb, and apply knowledge across the organization, 2) operational excellence – an ability to develop world-class systems and processes, and 3) relational excellence – an ability to work effectively with culturally diverse customers, colleagues, and partners.

▼ **USING AN INTRANET**
This manager is searching on the intranet to identify people in her organization who have the expertise to be part of a new global product development team.

POINTS TO REMEMBER

● Similarities in global customer preferences present opportunities for greater economies of scale.

● Global customers like to deal with suppliers who can fulfill their needs around the world.

● Focus attention on capabilities that make your organization distinctive in the global market.

MAXIMIZING VALUE AND MINIMIZING COSTS

A business consists of value-creating activities, such as product development and marketing. Your organization must decide where to locate each of these activities in order to maximize value creation and minimize costs. Allocate responsibilities and transform your business structure into a global network by putting procedures in place to coordinate areas such as budgeting and reporting.

MANAGING FOR RESULTS

One of your critical responsibilities as a global manager is to attract, develop, and retain world-class talent. Remember that talented workers are attracted to the worldwide business arena by the opportunity to perform challenging and creative work, and by the chance of professional development. They also value programs that reward results. Ensure that collaboration across borders is possible, and that your organization has processes for capturing, disseminating, and integrating new knowledge and best practices.

13 Remember that a talented workforce is crucial for global success.

▼ **PRIORITIZING PEOPLE**
Successful globalization depends on talented people. Employ the best people, extend their expertise, and give them the necessary incentives to stay with you.

Attract ▶ **Develop** ▶ **Retain**

ATTRACTING TOP-QUALITY EMPLOYEES

INCENTIVE	ADVANTAGE
CHALLENGING WORK	Well-designed jobs and international project assignments create a real sense of accomplishment and fulfillment.
FAMILY SUPPORT	Ongoing support enables staff and their families to manage the demands of living and working across borders.
GLOBAL OPPORTUNITIES	Work in different environments provides the opportunity to gain a rewarding global business perspective.
PROFESSIONAL DEVELOPMENT	Opportunities to gain cutting-edge skills and knowledge increase personal effectiveness and satisfaction.
REWARD AND RECOGNITION	Formal compensation programs and career advancement arrangements show that global experience is valued.
WORLD TRAVEL	Adventurous individuals appreciate the chance to explore the world and experience different cultures.

RENEWING FOR GROWTH

A business must work continually to create its own future in the global market. It does this by scanning the marketplace constantly and creating new opportunities beyond the current vision of the consumer. Make sure that your team of employees is diverse enough to cope with the challenge of a global market: remember that diversity promotes innovation. Ensure that your organizational culture is an incubator for top-quality ideas.

Team member suggests idea for how to develop a product

Manager reacts positively to new idea

---

14 Compare, assess, and rank your organization against its global competitors.

▲ **SHARING IDEAS**
This manager recognizes the value of fostering and sharing ideas. He arranges regular meetings where team members can express and discuss their views.

STAYING COMMITTED TO CORE VALUES

While it is important to be prepared to change in a dynamic global marketplace, it is also important to conserve what is of long-term value. A global organization needs to identify those features of its business that should not be changed or may be changed only very slowly. An organization's commitment to its core values, for example, will show its integrity and reliability to its customers and partners. These consistent values will also provide diverse stakeholders around the world with a clear view of what they can expect when dealing with your firm. Recognize that your successful global brands also need conserving – these help generate recognition and confidence.

THINGS TO DO

1. Share strategic information with staff worldwide.
2. Keep local managers involved in identifying global solutions.
3. Seek out and eliminate obstacles to global coordination.
4. Establish global performance indicators for the business.
5. Look for talented and creative staff.

IDENTIFYING PERSONAL SUCCESS FACTORS

The global manager must be flexible and open-minded. Be ready to adapt your habitual attitudes and behavior so that you can enjoy successful working relationships with people from other cultures and from different geographical locations.

15 Be open to advice from managers who have more global experience.

16 Learn about different cultures and lifestyles.

17 Believe in your abilities but be open to change.

MANAGING YOURSELF

Cosmopolitan attitudes are essential in global managers, who must behave as global citizens as well as national citizens. Learn how other cultures do business, and be prepared to adapt to altering circumstances. Think about ways you could approach new situations. Challenge your existing mental perceptions and biases, and be open to other people's points of view, even if they differ considerably from your own. Set realistic expectations for yourself and others when working across borders and persevere even in conditions of high uncertainty and ambiguity.

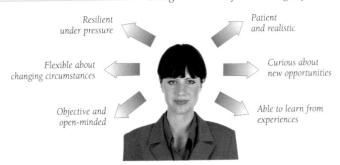

Resilient under pressure

Patient and realistic

Flexible about changing circumstances

Curious about new opportunities

Objective and open-minded

Able to learn from experiences

QUALITIES OF A GOOD GLOBAL MANAGER

MANAGING RELATIONSHIPS

Global managers need to collaborate effectively across borders so that they can develop synergies throughout the global business. Work at finding routes to shared understandings, despite language barriers and other cultural differences. Learn to see the world from the point of view of another culture. This, in turn, will enable you to build better relationships and increase your persuasiveness. It will also help you to recognize and adapt to different bargaining and conflict-management styles. Finally, create an extensive web of relationships inside and outside your organization and benefit from the support and knowledge you gain through them.

POINTS TO REMEMBER

● There will be gaps in your local management capabilities – analyze these honestly.

● Learning to manage successfully in a global economy is a continual process.

● It is important to be receptive to international opportunities and to be willing to take risks.

 18 Be an example to others in how to develop oneself.

DEVELOPING GLOBAL MANAGEMENT COMPETENCIES

TYPE OF APPROACH	ACTION
CONCEPTUALIZE	Identify patterns in the global environment that will help increase your understanding and effectiveness.
BUILD A CULTURE	Create an inclusive business culture in which people from diverse backgrounds can contribute their best work.
SCAN THE ENVIRONMENT	Detect and assess all possible risks and opportunities in the global marketplace.
INTEGRATE	Think beyond either/or answers to generate both/and solutions to complex problems.
OPTIMIZE	Look for a balance between global and local needs to generate the best possible results.
PARTNER	Discover potential alliances with competitors, related businesses, suppliers, and distributors.

MANAGING YOUR GLOBAL CAREER

A global career offers you numerous opportunities. Identify the different roles and options open to you and then devise a clear focus for your career. Aim to gain the necessary experiences you need so that you can form your career path.

19 Find a person with international experience to be your role model.

20 Let your boss know that you would like to take on international assignments.

LOOKING AT GLOBAL GENERALISTS

Usually located at the corporate center, global generalists have experience in a number of the organization's strategic businesses and markets worldwide. They understand how the businesses, customers, partners, suppliers, and distributors work together. Their role is primarily strategic and they make decisions based on their broad knowledge of global opportunities and risks. They are also responsible for ensuring that the next generation of global leaders is developed.

LOOKING AT GLOBAL SPECIALISTS

Global specialists are experts in their business or functional area. For example, they might be a global product manager or a global human resources manager. Typically based at the corporate center, they may complete assignments in local territories, bringing with them global knowledge and expertise. They may also act as integrators, identifying and transferring best practices worldwide. Their primary role is to ensure that the business operates to a world-class standard.

21 Develop a career plan and work toward realizing it.

22 Make continuous learning your top priority.

UNDERSTANDING LOCAL GENERALISTS

Country managers are experts in their territorial businesses and markets – they are known as local generalists. They need to understand how their operation fits into the total global enterprise. Key to aligning local and global strategies, they must make sure that the drive for global efficiencies is achievable and realistic at a local level. Given their pivotal role in translating global strategies into local tactics, they are in a strong position to become future global leaders.

▲ **KEEPING INFORMED**
A global manager needs firsthand knowledge of the way the business works at the local level, and to understand the perspective of local employees.

QUESTIONS TO ASK YOURSELF

Q What kind of global management career do I want?

Q How can I educate myself in international business?

Q What can I do to develop a network of global contacts in the organization?

UNDERSTANDING LOCAL SPECIALISTS

A factory manager, for example, is a local specialist – he or she is an expert within a local operation. While their primary focus is local, they are likely to deal with global processes. They may also be involved in regional or global teams, because they are able to supply a global business team with valuable insights about local issues.

GAINING THE RIGHT EXPERIENCE FOR YOUR CAREER

GENERALIST	SPECIALIST
GLOBAL	**GLOBAL**
● Take every chance to gain experience in different businesses and multiple markets.	● Look for ways to gain specific business, product, or functional expertise.
● Seek opportunities to develop expertise in strategic thinking.	● Apply your knowledge and skills in the organization's strategic markets.
LOCAL	**LOCAL**
● Gain multiple experiences within local businesses and functions.	● Become an expert in a local business, product, or function.
● Make the most of any opportunities to work on global teams.	● Make sure that you align yourself and your business with global standards.

MANAGING THE GLOBAL ASSIGNMENT

Global management careers involve a range of international assignments – short-, medium-, and long-term. Before a stint abroad, make sure that you prepare yourself properly so that you can adjust to what can be a dramatic change in lifestyle.

23 Avoid comparisons between your home and your host cultures.

24 Be honest with yourself about any fears that you have.

ADAPTING WELL ▼
To be able to cope in a new environment, be understanding, avoid preconceived notions, and be flexible.

PREPARING YOURSELF

To succeed on an international assignment, you must be able to accept that each culture makes sense to the people who live within it. Appreciate each culture's potential value, and be ready to integrate what is of value into your way of working. Learn about the culture you will be visiting by reading, seeking cross-cultural training, developing friendships with overseas colleagues, and traveling.

| Be respectful | → | Keep an open mind | → | Be ready to adapt |

Consultant briefs manager on etiquette and values

Listens attentively to experienced advice

Notes key points

◀ **SEEKING ADVICE**
Before an international assignment, this manager meets a consultant so that she can find out about the country she is visiting and be made aware of any potential difficulties.

▲ INVOLVING YOUR FAMILY
When you are about to embark on a long-term assignment abroad, remember that your whole family is affected and that you will all be making the move. Work together as you prepare for your trip.

CONSIDERING FAMILY

Before you and your family leave for a lengthy assignment abroad, it is vital that you are all well-informed. Make sure that your family members feel totally involved in preparations for moving and that you discuss any concerns that they may have. Prepare your family for differences in everyday life, such as shopping, transportation, postal services, and recreation. Find out about education and health care services in the country you will be living in. If you can, try to visit your host country with your family before committing yourself to going.

MAKING ADJUSTMENTS

While you are abroad, you may find that cultural differences cause frustration. You can fight, flee, or go with the flow. The latter will help you to see how the host culture operates. This enables you to make adjustments and begin to adapt. Help yourself adjust by regularly contacting friends at home. Get to know other expatriates and make a point of continuing ordinary family rituals.

25 Be adaptable, but be clear about the lines you are not prepared to cross.

THINGS TO DO

1. Set yourself modest goals and celebrate successes.
2. Share your thoughts and feelings with your family.
3. If you have a negative response to a new environment, avoid blaming the local culture.

RETURNING HOME

After the initial pleasure of getting home from a stint of work abroad, you may feel an anticlimax. You are not the same person that you were, time has not stood still at home, and, often, few people are interested in what you have done. Counter any disappointment with some adjustment strategies. At work, set up sessions to communicate what you have learned and to highlight any valuable practices used in the country you have been living in. Encourage your family to reflect on the experience of having lived abroad.

MANAGING RELATIONSHIPS

A global manager appreciates the impact that culture has on business. Aim to understand cultural differences, develop your relationship skills, and overcome communication barriers.

UNDERSTANDING CULTURE

Groups of people see the world through their own set of assumptions, beliefs, values, and attitudes. Learn about your culture and how it has shaped you, and aim to understand how other cultures work so that you can be an effective global manager.

26 View a difficult cross-cultural interaction as part of a learning curve.

27 Experiment with new routines and rituals.

28 Be aware of your cultural habits and assumptions.

WHAT IS CULTURE?

Culture may be defined as the inherited ideas, beliefs, values, and knowledge of a group. As well as providing a sense of shared identity and belonging, culture helps us solve three types of problems: physical (how we feed, clothe, and shelter ourselves); philosophical (the meaning and purpose of life, and understandings about right and wrong); and relational (how we behave toward other members of our group and with other groups). Remember that our cultural solutions to these problems are learned, not innate, and are passed on through generations.

CULTURAL INFLUENCES

As a cultural group, our solutions to life's fundamental questions are influenced greatly by the natural environment in which we live, and our history, religion, and language. Individually, a mixture of formal and informal influences shapes us. Look at how national, local, organizational, professional, and functional cultures all have an effect on our outlook. National influences include institutions like the family, schools, churches, peer groups, and the media. Organizational influences include value statements, policies and procedures, and reward and recognition systems.

▲ **DIFFERENT CULTURES**
Culture influences every aspect of our lives – from the way we dress to the way we conduct business.

29 Remain open-minded, flexible, and ready to learn – even when other people are not.

ANALYZING CULTURES

Cultures are often said to be like icebergs. Above the surface are the characteristics that can be seen, heard, touched, smelled, and tasted, such as food, dress, art, and the use of gestures. Below the surface are the largely unconscious assumptions, attitudes, and beliefs that shape decision-making, relationships, conflict, and so on. Recognize that it is the below-the-surface aspects that cause the most problems when doing business across borders.

UNDERSTANDING CULTURES

Your first challenge is to become aware of the reality of cultural diversity. Next, you must develop appropriate attitudes for working cross-culturally – including respect, openness, and a willingness to learn. Seek knowledge of other cultures through firsthand experience and/or research. Translate your knowledge into specific skills that you will be able to use, such as international negotiation techniques and leading global teams.

BARRIERS TO CULTURAL COMMUNICATION

There are many factors that can be a barrier to cross-cultural communication:
● A belief that we are all the same.
● A perception that you have nothing to learn from others.
● An attitude that your way is best.
● The opinion that those who are culturally different to you need to be developed.

IDENTIFYING CULTURAL PATTERNS

The shared assumptions, values, and beliefs of a group form a cultural pattern. Teach yourself how the pattern fits together – its underlying logic – so that you can adapt to new environments quickly and effectively in your role as a global manager.

30 Start by understanding, and being honest with, yourself.

31 Learn as much as you can about other cultures.

32 Get to know individuals from other cultures.

CULTURAL COMPLEXITY

Although each culture is unique and complex, being made up of internal tensions, contradictions, and variations, it is possible to identify three main cultural "types" – autonomy, consensus, and status. Cultural types are very broad generalizations and should be treated with caution. They are useful guides, but they must be open to modification: If they are used to form stereotypes, they become destructive. Avoid allowing stereotypes to block your sensitivity to, and understanding of, individual exceptions.

RECOGNIZING AUTONOMY CULTURES

Members of autonomy cultures seek individuality and independence. A person in this type of culture is expected to determine his or her own identity, and dependence on other individuals or institutions is seen as a weakness. Conformity is expected only to the degree that it allows the society to function with some cohesion. Areas associated with this cultural type include Australia and New Zealand, Canada and the United States, and many parts of northern and western Europe.

POINTS TO REMEMBER

● In reality, cultures are a unique mix of cultural types, although one type will tend to be dominant.

● Study and careful observation are needed to help you understand a culture.

● The internet is a useful resource for cultural information.

● The more time you spend in a different culture, the more complex it will appear.

UNDERSTANDING CONSENSUS CULTURES

Members of consensus cultures are driven by the need for harmony, at least on the surface. The individual's personal identity is closely bound to that of a larger group, which maintains its identity by encouraging homogeneity and conformity. Great importance is placed on stability within the group. Becoming alienated from it can be very traumatic for the individual. Many parts of Asia have consensus-type cultures, including Japan, and, to a lesser extent, China and Korea.

33 Note that not all cultures work in the same way.

34 Inspire others to learn about different cultures.

35 Treat every model of culture as a generalized idea, not a fixed reality.

OPENING YOUR MIND ▼
A manager who refuses to learn and listen has a very limited view of the world. He must develop a more cosmopolitan and open-minded outlook.

IDENTIFYING STATUS CULTURES

Honor and respect, both for the individual and the group, drive members of status cultures. In this type of culture, an individual's identity is closely connected to that of the group, which can be an extended family, class, clan, or tribe. The shared heritage of group members is important: Group survival and pride are of supreme value. Loyalty to strong leaders who are representative of the group is essential. Areas associated with status-type cultures include southern Europe, South America, Africa, and the Middle East.

This manager has fixed opinions and is not open to other people's views

When he notices himself behaving in this way, he tries to stop himself from making quick judgments based on his own cultural assumptions

He finds that by listening to others, he can find new inspiration and ideas

ADAPTING TO CULTURAL DIFFERENCES

Global managers must realize that many of the business practices which work successfully in their home culture will not be appropriate in another country. Ensure that you are able to adjust your approach to suit different cultural contexts.

36 Find a middle path between being yourself and adapting to others.

37 Respect and use the customary formalities that are valued by your host culture.

ADAPTING SUCCESSFULLY

To be effective, you need to be able to adapt in a new environment. However, adaptation does not equal adoption. For example, you are not trying to switch from being English to being Italian – this would make you appear foolish and manipulative. Adapt to show respect for another culture and to build relationships. For example, in a consensus culture, communicate in an indirect way, because this will make your hosts feel most comfortable.

SUCCEEDING IN CONSENSUS CULTURES

Relationships and long-term business goals are important in consensus cultures. Invest time in building lasting relationships and respect the formalities. For example, do not make someone "lose face" by criticizing them in public. Be patient and do not try to rush decisions. Also, be prepared for questions about yourself and your organization.

Accepts business card

SHOWING RESPECT ▶
In this example, a manager greets someone from a consensus culture by offering his card. He does not realize that it is respectful to offer a card using both hands.

SUCCEEDING IN AUTONOMY CULTURES

Members of autonomy cultures tend to be pragmatic, task-focused, and driven by quick results. They will like you to be flexible, but also decisive and action-oriented. Try to demonstrate optimism, confidence, and initiative when you are in this environment. Show how you can help individuals reach their goals, by selling yourself and your ideas. Time is money in such cultures, so be punctual and meet deadlines.

38 Be prepared to work outside the comfort zone and customs of your own culture.

SUCCEEDING IN STATUS CULTURES

Business in status cultures is usually highly personal. Work at building trust, and show respect for your colleagues and your superiors. Be aware that a hierarchy exists and be careful not to cause unintentional offense. Always accept hospitality, because it is tied to honor. Expect lots of small talk – get down to business only when your counterpart gives you some cues. Expect many interruptions and be patient. Stay focused on timing rather than timekeeping.

CULTURAL DIFFERENCES

Some issues that you take for granted may be viewed very differently in another culture. Where different cultural expectations are not properly understood, deals can be lost and products can fail. For example, in Africa it is customary to illustrate food packaging using an image of the product inside. Thus it is inappropriate to put a picture of a baby on a jar of baby food.

▼ **RESPECTING CULTURES**
In this example, a manager working in a different culture to his own found that his assumptions about acceptable behavior were challenged. He adjusted accordingly.

CASE STUDY
An Englishman working in a status culture in Europe saw some inefficiencies in his department's processes. He decided to take the initiative and so he produced a report on what he saw as the department's problems and he suggested some solutions.
When he presented the report to his boss, he expected some praise and encouragement. Instead, his boss glared angrily, and over the next several weeks, treated him with suspicion.
A colleague pointed out to the Englishman that he had insulted his boss. Within a status culture, the boss is perceived to be the expert, the problem solver. It was as if the Englishman had said to his boss, "You're not doing your job properly!" Next time the Englishman noticed an issue, he subtly brought it to the attention of his boss – who then saw him as an ally.

DEVELOPING RELATIONSHIP ADVANTAGE

A vital challenge for the global manager is to build good working relationships across geographical and cultural borders. Recognize that strong, trusting relationships are the foundation of successful collaborations in a diverse business network.

39 Develop a strategy for building strong global relationships.

QUESTIONS TO ASK YOURSELF

Q Can I improve the way I communicate with customers from different cultures?

Q Do I understand the different cultural expectations of my global business partners?

Q Do I have good relationships with colleagues from around the globe?

IDENTIFYING ADVANTAGES

You can gain advantage over your competitors in three main ways. The first is in intellectual capital, such as knowledge and copyrights. The second is in operational systems, including best processes and systems. The third is in relationships – the ability to develop strong personal and group links across geographical, business, and cultural borders. Be aware that relationship advantage is very difficult for a competitor to replicate. Good feeling across the global network cannot be manufactured.

DEVELOPING PARTNERSHIPS

Global businesses are dependent on their ability to forge international joint ventures and alliances. Most partnerships fail because of cultural neglect. Too many managers assume that if the economics look good, success is guaranteed. Beyond studying the spreadsheets, be prepared to develop cultural understanding. Let go of "there is only one way" thinking and shift from "either/or" to "both/and" working methods, to create business methods that give the best results for all parties. Encourage others on your team to do the same.

THINGS TO DO

1. Think about your global relationships – customers, partners, and colleagues.
2. Identify their needs.
3. Implement initiatives to meet these needs.
4. Review these relationships regularly to make sure that they are working well.

FOCUSING ON COLLEAGUES

Global organizations aim to draw on the talent and expertise within their worldwide networks. New initiatives in product development, marketing, and delivery are often dependent on cross-border collaboration. Many businesses also expect fresh perspectives to be generated through their diverse employees. Make sure that employees around the world are able to share ideas.

40 Learn to see your organization's products in the same way that your diverse customers do.

BLENDING DIFFERENCES ▶
Create a culture of inclusion in which differences are respected, but are not the primary focus. Instead, use these differences to create value for customers and the business.

> Meet your partners and agree on shared business objectives

> Identify tasks that need to be done to meet those objectives

> Identify how each culture would carry out those tasks

> Analyze the advantages of each approach in a specific context

> Decide on the best approach, or mix of approaches, to use

CONNECTING WITH THE CUSTOMER

It is vital to understand your customers in their cultural context. Only by learning what factors influence their diverse perceptions of value, quality, and service is your business able to develop products that will meet their needs. For example, cost is a key concern to customers in northern Europe, but not to such an extent in Latin America, where people are more interested in value. In southern Europe and Asia, high levels of service will encourage repeat purchases, but will not have the same effect in northern Europe. Standardization must be balanced with responsiveness to local conditions. For example, a global hamburger chain opened a kosher restaurant in Jerusalem, and used lamb instead of beef in India.

RESEARCHING CUSTOMER VALUES ▶
Your customers hold the key to your organization's success as a global competitor. Gather data so that you can begin to build a picture of your customers in all your different markets.

MANAGING YOURSELF

To be a successful global manager, you must learn to manage yourself successfully. Be aware of your typical responses to a variety of situations, and start to develop those responses that increase your managerial effectiveness.

41 Remind yourself of other adaptations you have made in your life.

ANALYZING YOURSELF

Commit yourself to self-understanding

⬇

Detach yourself from your perceptions of "yourself"

⬇

Observe yourself in action in different contexts

⬇

Analyze your ways of thinking, feeling, and behaving

⬇

Create new options that increase your adaptability

⬇

Aim to act deliberately, instead of habitually

MANAGING FEELINGS

Working across cultures can trigger a range of intense feelings: fear, superiority, helplessness, anger, anxiety, disgust. If these influence your work and interaction with others, they can be destructive. Acknowledge them, compartmentalize them, and examine them objectively. Remember that tasks can be repeated and decisions reversed, but relationships are very difficult to repair.

QUESTIONS TO ASK YOURSELF

Q How do I think and act in new situations?

Q How do I handle difficult situations?

Q Would these strategies work for me in all cultures?

Q What causes me the most stress and why?

Q Have I had positive feedback that I could act upon?

Q How can I increase my self-awareness?

MANAGING THOUGHTS

Everyone learns thought patterns that provide shortcuts to understanding. Stereotyping, where we sort the world into categories and put new information into one of these, is an example. Learn to manage your thinking so that you can handle greater complexity. Resist taking shortcuts – and making quick, often false, assumptions – and learn to tolerate different situations and beliefs.

MANAGING BEHAVIORS

Awareness of the underlying cultural influence in how you speak and behave is a critical step toward self-management. If you are from a culture that values hierarchy, you will communicate some form of deference in your speech and body language. Realize that although this is acceptable in your home environment, your deference may be perceived as weakness when you work in a culture that values an open, democratic leadership. In this new context, manage your behavior by becoming more assertive and explicit so that you increase your effectiveness.

42 Ask someone to comment on your behavioral traits.

43 Set yourself small goals and work to achieve them.

◀ **BEING AWARE OF BODY LANGUAGE**
This manager's open gestures may create an impression of honesty and friendliness in a Western culture. However, it may be viewed as disrespectful in Asian cultures.

ANALYZING YOUR SELF-MANAGEMENT CAPABILITIES

CAPABILITY	POSITIVE ASPECTS	NEGATIVE ASPECTS
MANAGING FEELINGS	● Able to handle stress ● Optimistic, self-confident ● Good self-awareness ● Flexible and cooperative	● Always on guard and abrasive ● Cynical ● Judgmental and self-righteous ● Ethnocentric
MANAGING THINKING	● Reflects on experience ● Quick thinking and creative ● Honest and nonconformist ● Able to improvise	● Tendency toward denial ● Not a team player ● Egotistical and gullible ● Needs definite answers
MANAGING BEHAVIOR	● Observes and listens ● Sociable and easy going ● Patient and realistic ● Criticizes constructively	● Averse to risks ● Fearful of losing face ● Needs to be in control ● Unable to criticize self

BUILDING GLOBAL RELATIONSHIPS

Strong relationships are built on trust and influence wherever you are in the world. Focus on developing trust, and show interest in and respect for other cultures. Learn to see the world from the perspective of other cultures, rather than just your own.

44 Ask yourself: "Am I reading this behavior correctly?"

45 Notice which communication channels your colleagues prefer, and use them.

FORMING RELATIONSHIPS

Culture affects how quickly relationships can be formed and what obligations are assumed from these relationships. In European cultures, where mobility has traditionally been low, communities are guarded about sharing personal information: Relationships tend to be formed slowly. Trust is only earned over time. In mobile societies like the United States, relationships tend to be developed quickly before people move on.

DEVELOPING TRUST

It is vital not to misread cultural signals, because this can undermine trust. In the office, character, competence, and confidence are key to trust, but it is possible to misread signals in these areas:

● Character – people who are used to explicit communication can confuse indirectness with lying and begin questioning someone's integrity.

● Competence – in some cultures, family connections influence position, but this doesn't mean that these managers lack expertise.

● Confidence – an individualist working with someone from a harmony-driven culture might confuse modesty with weakness.

QUESTIONS TO ASK YOURSELF

Q What do people in this culture expect of a relationship?

Q Are relationships in this culture traditionally built quickly or slowly?

Q What will make a good impression?

Q Is trust assumed, or must it be earned over time?

Q What needs to be done in order to keep the relationship strong?

SHOWING INTEREST

A quick way to build relationships is to show a genuine interest in the other person's culture. Many Westerners focus on getting work done, and only then – time allowing – work at building relationships. To other cultures, this appears impersonal. Typically, people everywhere are happy to talk about their culture. When you are on a business trip, show an interest in your surroundings. For example, "On the way from the airport, I saw people singing and dancing. Can you tell me what the festival is about?"

46 Keep a record of your contacts in the global network.

47 Make relationship-building a pleasure, not a task.

48 Keep in touch with colleagues – do not wait for a business need.

DEVELOPING NETWORKS

Global organizations depend on deep and strong collaboration across borders. Consider sponsoring cross-border events, such as training workshops. Think about creating global bulletin boards on the intranet, where people can share international experiences. Intranets are useful for producing learning modules on cultural awareness, and for networking and teamwork.

ASSESSING COMMUNICATION STYLES

COMMUNICATION STYLE	ADVANTAGES
MEETING FACE TO FACE	It is helpful to gauge people's feelings through their body language and facial expressions. Strong relationships can result.
VIDEO-CONFERENCING	The technology allows members of the global business to discuss issues in real time and put names to faces with their overseas colleagues.
CONVERSING BY TELEPHONE	Talking to overseas colleagues, instead of corresponding in writing, ensures that any misunderstandings can be clarified instantly.

UNDERSTANDING CROSS-CULTURAL COMMUNICATION

Some cultures communicate most readily via written messages, while others prefer talking. To relate successfully, understand what communication is, how it works, and how to tailor it to the cultural context into which it will be received.

49 Create the right conditions for open cross-cultural dialogue.

QUESTIONS TO ASK YOURSELF

Q Who should be communicating and with whom?

Q What information should the message contain?

Q How should it be designed for the best effect?

Q When is the best time to send the message?

Q Where is the best place to deliver it?

UNDERSTANDING COMMUNICATION

When we "deliver" a message, we assume that we have "communicated." But it is often the case that what has been said is not the same as what has been heard. Although the communicator may feel in control, it is the receiver who determines whether communication takes place. Remember that the outcome of successful communication is agreement about meaning. This can be difficult to achieve in cross-cultural communication where some degree of misunderstanding is inevitable.

MODELING COMMUNICATION

In a simple model of communication, a sender encodes a message using symbols, words, pictures, and/or gestures. It is then sent to the receiver via a message channel (face to face, telephone, e-mail). The receiver decodes the message (interprets its meaning). Typically, the receiver sends a message back to the sender, and becomes the encoder. The original sender becomes the decoder. Be aware of cultural influences in how the sender encodes the message and how the receiver decodes it.

50 Always check for shared understanding.

51 Remember, talking louder does not help understanding.

CULTURAL DIFFERENCES

In relationship-focused cultures, such as those in Asia, words only convey a small part of the message; the listener infers the rest, based on their knowledge of the speaker, the setting of the conversation, and any body language. Task-focused cultures such as Germany or the United States, prefer to use words as the key form of communication.

UNDERSTANDING COMMUNICATION STYLES

Autonomy cultures prefer explicit and precise communication, with little use of body language. Consensus cultures tend to be more indirect: meaning depends on the wider context, such as who says what to whom. In status cultures, communication tends to be rhetorical and emotional, using exaggeration and repetition.

52 Make sure that your intent is to learn from communication, rather than to compete or control.

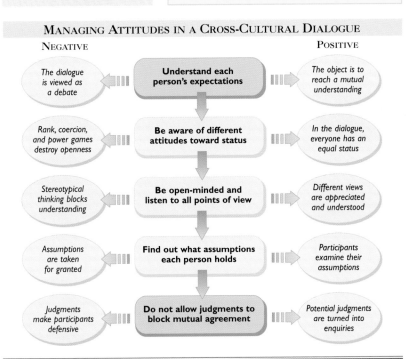

MANAGING ATTITUDES IN A CROSS-CULTURAL DIALOGUE

NEGATIVE		POSITIVE
The dialogue is viewed as a debate	**Understand each person's expectations**	The object is to reach a mutual understanding
Rank, coercion, and power games destroy openness	**Be aware of different attitudes toward status**	In the dialogue, everyone has an equal status
Stereotypical thinking blocks understanding	**Be open-minded and listen to all points of view**	Different views are appreciated and understood
Assumptions are taken for granted	**Find out what assumptions each person holds**	Participants examine their assumptions
Judgments make participants defensive	**Do not allow judgments to block mutual agreement**	Potential judgments are turned into enquiries

OVERCOMING COMMUNICATION BARRIERS

The barriers to communicating across cultures must be recognized and managed. Be aware of all the pitfalls of communication so that you avoid sending or receiving the wrong messages, and always try to see other people's points of view.

53 Empathize with your foreign colleague's needs and wants.

54 Always consider whether your body language is helping or hindering a discussion.

MISINTERPRETING SIGNS

It is easy to misinterpret someone's behavior by assuming that they share our understanding of it. For example, many Westerners interpret direct eye contact during conversation as a sign of sincerity, whereas in Asian cultures, a lowering of the eyes communicates respectful deference. The Asian may consider the Westerner's behavior as aggressive, even hostile, while the Westerner sees the Asian's behavior as insincere. The result – instant distrust between the parties.

READING BODY LANGUAGE

Along with eye contact, body movement (facial expressions, gestures, handshakes, bows, and posture) is an important form of nonverbal communication. People from all cultures use their bodies to reinforce the meaning of what they say, to communicate something that they have not said, or even to oppose what they are saying. Be aware of your body language and learn about the body language used in other cultures. For example, pointing a finger to emphasize a point can be seen as rude, rather than emphatic, in some Asian cultures.

Two managers are involved in heated debate

AVOIDING ETHNOCENTRISM

Making the standards of one's own group – what is considered right, reasonable, and rational – the standards for the rest of the world, is known as ethnocentrism. It is usually accompanied with feelings of superiority. Everyone experiences ethnocentric feelings. Acknowledge them for what they are: destructive responses to the unfamiliar. Stay constructive and try to see things from the other person's point of view. Ask yourself: "What is causing such a strong reaction in me?" and "Am I being objective?" Look for what is interesting and valuable in the way the other person sees things.

55 Stay open to an issue, even if it appears to go against your values.

Mutual understanding is reached

He realizes that they are both ultimately aiming for same goal

Manager considers colleague's point of view

Managers will not listen to each other's reasoning

Communication breaks down completely

◀ **SHOWING UNDERSTANDING**
In this example, two managers are arguing about how to deal with a procedure and their conversation is quickly deteriorating. To try to prevent the discussion from breaking down in animosity, the managers need to follow the golden rule of communication: Listen first, think second, and then talk.

RECOGNIZING GENDER ISSUES

Manager greets customer warmly

It is widely thought that women face more prejudice than men in the international workplace. In fact, many women report a "halo effect" when working in some male-dominated cultures. The men recognize that women managers are rare, and so think those that do exist must be outstanding. However, remember that some cultures demarcate strongly between male and female roles and this can make it difficult for women to succeed.

BUILDING RELATIONSHIPS ▶
It has been suggested that women are more successful than men in international business because they pay more attention to building and maintaining positive relationships.

POINTS TO REMEMBER

- Keep your language simple and only present one idea at a time.
- If you do not understand a point, do not pretend that you do.
- Be prepared to ask questions.
- If you make a telephone call, follow it up with an email.
- Speak slowly and clearly.

USING CLEAR LANGUAGE

The key to communication is to put yourself in your reader's or listener's place, while paying attention to some basics. Be careful to avoid slang, jargon, acronyms, buzzwords, clichés, and colloquialisms. Make sure that you are literal and specific; vague, abstract language will confuse and frustrate your customer or colleague. Provide adequate contextual information. Do not simply count on others knowing what you mean.

WOMEN WORKING GLOBALLY

Women working on an assignment in a different culture to their own can be faced with a variety of challenges. There are ways to help overcome any potential difficulties:

- Find a consultant who can brief you on values and norms of behavior.
- Display professionalism in how you dress and respect local customs.

- Be very well prepared in all aspects of your work and make your presentations direct, with few qualifiers.
- Demonstrate your decision-making power and authority.
- Do not take male-dominated cultures personally or react to them by becoming aggressive.

BEING SENSITIVE

A general rule in successful communication is to stay clear of subjects such as sex, politics, and religion until trust is established. Initially, discuss neutral topics like your journey, the weather, and vacations. Wait until you know someone better before talking about families. Take your cue from them as to when this might be appropriate.

A sense of humor enables you to put your cultural mistakes into perspective. However, beware: jokes rarely translate well, because they often rely on local knowledge.

56 Avoid potentially controversial topics at the beginning of a relationship.

BEING PREPARED ▶
In this example, an American businessman realized that he needed to adapt his behavior and body language in order to gain respect and achieve success in a different culture.

CASE STUDY
An American businessman visited a bank in Tokyo. He walked into the meeting room and threw himself into his chair. He sat back and crossed his legs casually. The Japanese bankers said nothing but exchanged quick glances with one another. They knew instantly that their bank would not want to do business with this rude man.
Realizing his mistake, the next time the American

businessman planned a trip to Japan, he took the time to learn about Japanese habits and manners.
When he arrived in Japan, he greeted his hosts with a small bow and exchanged business cards with both hands. He sat formally in his chair and did not rush to talk about business, but discussed his trip and his interest in Japanese current affairs. He also exchanged small gifts with his hosts. He was received positively.

57 Keep your sense of humor, but leave your jokes at home.

58 Make your interpretations tentative until they are confirmed.

AVOIDING STEREOTYPES

Stereotypes are relatively fixed generalizations made about others and they leave little room for identifying and adapting to individual differences. Stereotypes can be negative ("all … are lazy") or positive ("all … are smart"). Both types are empty statements with no value. One of the most important tasks facing any global manager is to examine your, largely unconscious, stereotypes. Any generalizations that you do make must be very tentative and open to change. Keep in mind that you do not interact with a whole culture, but with individuals from within it.

MANAGING GLOBAL ETHICS

Globalization increases our exposure to different ethical norms. Be sensitive to other people's cultural perceptions of what is right or wrong, and understand the systems your organization has for dealing with ethical issues.

> **59** Be clear about your own moral values – and adhere to them.

Manager studies international law book

▲ STUDYING THE LAW
Make yourself fully aware of how your organization views ethical matters. Read up on the legal situation at home and abroad.

STUDYING ETHICS

Ethics is about morality – identifying acceptable standards of conduct. There are many daunting ethical issues that a global manager might have to deal with, including payments made to foreign officials or businesses to win contracts, insider trading, employee discrimination, environmental abuse, labor conditions, piracy, and counterfeiting. Seek help at corporate and local levels to deal with these. Make sure that you understand the legal framework of your home culture, and the ethical codes of your organization. Never rush to judgment. Be sure that you appreciate fully the potential consequences of any action you may take, for the business and for those involved.

AVOIDING IMPERIALISM

Perceptions of right and wrong vary. Bribery in one culture may be seen in another as the price for doing business. In one country, hiring relatives may be perceived as the rational thing to do (relatives can usually be trusted), whereas in another it would be considered nepotism. Even if general agreement exists on values such as human rights and environmental protection, specific definitions and overall priorities will differ. Avoid trying to impose your own standards because this may lead to accusations of ethical imperialism.

> **60** Make sure your organization has ethical guidelines.

> **61** Study examples of previous ethical dilemmas.

QUESTIONS TO ASK YOURSELF

Q Am I comfortable with living with the results of this action?

Q What if everyone acted in this way?

Q Would I want my children to do this?

Q Would I want this to happen to my family?

Q Would I want my family to see this in the newspaper?

ANALYZING OPTIONS

You can deal with ethical issues with either absolutism or relativism. In reality, ethical issues are complex, and solutions are not either/or. Applying absolute principles may have unintended results. For example, some American businesses withdrew their manufacturing sites from Bangladesh because of the use of child labor. Fearing the loss of more business, the factory owners dismissed 30–50,000 children. Many of these children then went into more dangerous jobs. Always look at a situation from several viewpoints.

BEING PROACTIVE

Organizations should be proactive in ethical issues, creating specific codes of conduct. These need to be reinforced by being included in performance evaluations and promotion criteria. Use training to introduce employees to different ethical norms and your organization's ethical expectations. If violations do occur, carry out an audit to find the causes – organizational culture, ineffective leadership, or inadequate reporting procedures may all be underlying problems.

62 Remember that good ethics lead to good business.

▼ USING TRAINING

Discuss a selection of ethical dilemmas likely to be encountered in global business with your team.

Colleague queries contentious issue

Manager outlines ethical policies

Key facts are noted on board

WORKING PRACTICES

When you begin working globally, all your managerial techniques will need to be adapted. Be prepared to adopt new practices to achieve your goals in a multicultural environment.

ASSESSING LEADERSHIP

Each culture has a perspective on what it means to be a good leader. Understand the different leadership styles that you may encounter, study respected leaders in other cultures, and be ready to adapt your leadership styles in different contexts.

63 Remember that one leadership style will not be appropriate for all.

64 Find a balance between tasks and relationships so that you can lead effectively.

ASSESSING POWER

How much power a leader has, and how it is used, varies between different cultures. In autonomy cultures, it is distributed widely – the hierarchy in organizations tends to be relatively flat. Decision-making is bottom-up and top-down, and everyone can contribute ideas and opinions. In consensus and status cultures, power is concentrated in a few hands, and there is a large gap between those who have power and those who do not. In these cultures, decision-making is top-down, although input may be gathered from employees who are lower down in the hierarchy.

THE PEOPLE DIMENSION OF LEADERSHIP

In autonomy cultures, leaders often have technical expertise and an impersonal approach. They tend to focus on the task to be done and rely on processes and action plans. Relationships are more important to leaders in consensus and status cultures, because they believe these will help get the job done. Leaders in consensus cultures take advice from the wider group and offer guidance. In status cultures, leaders are often strong, charismatic figures who rely on a close group of advisers.

65 Develop leaders in all levels and areas of your business.

66 Find someone to be your leadership mentor.

POINTS TO REMEMBER

- You should aim to lead your team with vision.
- Your team will be better focused if you provide it with a clear strategy.
- Learn what influencing techniques will be most effective in a particular culture and keep this in mind when you form a strategy.

IDENTIFYING STYLES

After taking into account the influence of power and relationships, research has identified four major leadership styles worldwide. The democratic leader provides a structure, consults widely, and empowers others. The collaborative leader becomes involved as a team player and negotiates shared solutions. The autocratic leader controls, and demands loyalty. The paternalistic leader is a parental figure, looking after the group's interests.

FLEXING STYLES

To get the best out of people, find out about their expectations of leadership. Employees who are used to an autocratic or paternalistic style of leadership may get confused if you use a more democratic style. To them, you may appear to lack authority and confidence. Make sure that you can adapt while also appearing and feeling natural.

PRACTICING STYLES ▶

This manager is receiving advice from a consultant about leadership styles: he is practicing leading democratically.

Manager role plays democratic style of leading

Consultant takes notes on his style

MOTIVATING ACROSS CULTURES

A global manager needs to identify the needs of individual employees, within the context of the culture in which he or she is working. Recognize the personal priorities of the diverse individuals in your team and apply the appropriate motivational tools.

67 Take note – the factors that motivate someone can change.

68 Remember that money is not the main motivator for everyone – family may be the priority.

FOCUSING ON MOTIVATION

People worldwide work to satisfy their needs and wants. These vary according to the circumstances of the individual, and on factors such as cultural values. It is difficult to generalize, but research suggests that professionals in a range of countries value challenge, autonomy, and the opportunities to use their skills. Not surprisingly, lower level workers place high importance on security, earnings, benefits, and working conditions. Make sure that you are sensitive to the different priorities of the individuals in your global team.

RECOGNIZING MOTIVATION

Beyond personal circumstances, individuals are influenced by wider cultural values. For example, in Latin America, job status and a good personal life are key motivators. In Saudi Arabia, family esteem is more important than public recognition. In one country, a job may be viewed as an economic necessity; in another country it may be tied to self-identity. Be aware of the values of different cultures.

▼ **MATERIAL POSSESSIONS**
Some people are motivated by expensive material possessions to show that they are successful in their work and have achieved a high standard of living.

LOOKING AT A MODEL OF MOTIVATION

This model of motivation focuses on the three basic needs that occur in any workforce. These are: the desire to achieve independence and personal accomplishment; the wish to affiliate and attain harmony; and the desire to have power and control decisions. These general motivations must then be looked at in the context of particular cultures:

- Autonomy cultures tend to be motivated by the desire to achieve.
- Consensus cultures are usually motivated by the wish to gain affiliation.
- Status cultures are often motivated by the desire for power.

To understand fully what motivates an individual, take personal circumstances into account and allow for cultural changes.

69 Ensure that you fit the right motivator to the culture and the individual.

USING TOOLS

Local knowledge enables a manager to determine the best motivators in the culture. In autonomy cultures, individual incentives are the most suitable. Use praise, promotions, and pay raises. In consensus cultures, group-based incentives work best. Distribute bonuses, formal recognition, competitive awards, and vacation awards throughout the team. Recognize that anything that enhances respect is motivational in status cultures – these include titles, position, flattery, gifts for the individual and the family, and bonuses.

DOS AND DON'TS

✔ Do ensure that your reward programs suit local cultural values.

✔ Do monitor the priorities of your employees, and make adjustments.

✘ Don't assume that the same things motivate all groups in a country.

✘ Don't assume that what has motivated people in the past will motivate them now.

THINKING ABOUT MOTIVATION

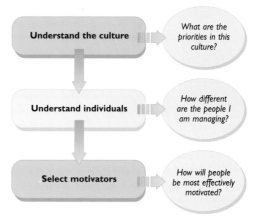

Understand the culture → What are the priorities in this culture?

Understand individuals → How different are the people I am managing?

Select motivators → How will people be most effectively motivated?

GIVING FEEDBACK

Managers need to give and receive feedback on performance. There are various methods for providing feedback, some more direct than others. Choose the appropriate method, depending on the culture in which it is being received.

70 Observe how other people in the culture give feedback.

DISCUSSING PERFORMANCE

Formal, direct feedback is typical in autonomy cultures. The focus is on the performance and personal strengths of the individual. Use two-way communication so that the employee can give his or her point of view and negotiate new goals. Bear in mind that autonomy cultures vary in their directness. In Britain and the United States, for example, encouraging words are said at the beginning and end of a performance review. In Germany, criticism is more direct.

Manager discusses employee's views

▲ **COMMUNICATING OPENLY**
Feedback in an autonomy culture is expected to be an exchange of views and a negotiation of new goals. Both sides will communicate equally.

Manager gives her thoughts on employee's project

ONE-WAY FEEDBACK

Performance feedback in status cultures tends to be spontaneous and only one way: Two-way communications could undermine the authority of the manager. Reputation is critical so some problems may need to be skirted around to prevent a manager appearing to have failed. Negative feedback could be conveyed via an intermediary. As well as performance, emphasize the employee's characteristics, including civility and loyalty.

◄ **STATING VIEWS**
Managers in status cultures tend to give feedback and express their opinions on the spur of the moment, rather than initiating a formal review session.

BEING INDIRECT

Indirect feedback is common in consensus cultures where preserving reputation, or "face," is critical. The manager counsels and guides. Feedback is likely to be relatively informal and continuous, with its focus being on how well an employee performs in the team. Try to speak to a group rather than an individual, tell hypothetical stories about oneself to illustrate a problem, and increase a person's responsibilities to show your approval.

71 Be careful to avoid causing someone embarrassment.

▼ ADDRESSING A GROUP
To help someone save face, feedback may be given to the whole group, rather than solely to an individual.

Manager gives critical feedback to whole group

Employee listens to feedback, but has not lost face in front of his colleagues

SAVING "FACE"

Face is an individual's reputation, the degree of respect in which he is held by others (known as *kao* in Japanese and *mianzi* in Chinese). There are a number of things you can say to prevent someone from losing face during a difficult debate or negotiation:

❝ *I didn't want to say anything in the meeting, but perhaps we could have a word in private.* ❞

❝ *Perhaps we could save that question until we have all had a chance to look at the specifications.* ❞

❝ *You should be very proud of your company. It has a wonderful history of reliability and customer service.* ❞

❝ *Let's not look to assign blame to anyone. We will solve this together through patience and goodwill.* ❞

MAKING PRESENTATIONS

Global managers are often called upon to make presentations to customers, employees, and joint venture partners. To give a successful presentation, make sure that you know your audience, and be clear about your key message and objectives.

72 Make it easy for your audience to understand your key points.

QUESTIONS TO ASK YOURSELF

Q Do I know my audience and what they will expect of me?

Q Am I clear about what I want to communicate?

Q Am I able to adapt if I am losing the audience's attention?

Q Should I have my presentation translated or use a translator?

ASSESSING AN AUDIENCE

Imagine your presentation as it will be seen by your audience. Consider the following points: the potential benefits your presentation offers them; how they will perceive you; what they will think of the subject matter; their cultural expectations about presentations. The more you know about your audience, the more confident you will be in delivering your message. Do not, however, let confidence appear as arrogance.

PLANNING PRESENTATIONS

A successful presentation needs to connect with the needs and wants of those who are going to be listening to it. Find out about the business situation of members of the audience, their cultural values, and what they will see as the benefits of working with you – such as cost, suitability for their culture, proven reliability, and long-term perspective. Identify your key messages and link them to these benefits in a logical sequence. Choose a presentation style that is appropriate for your intended audience, for example, adjust it to be formal or informal.

FORMING A STRUCTURE ▶
Give your presentation a structure, but research where the emphasis is required. North Americans, for example, will prefer you to get to the point without too much background information.

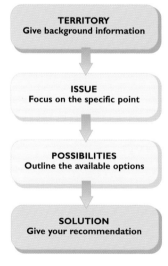

TERRITORY
Give background information

ISSUE
Focus on the specific point

POSSIBILITIES
Outline the available options

SOLUTION
Give your recommendation

USING TOOLS AT A PRESENTATION

TOOL	HOW TO APPLY
PRESENTATION MAP	At the outset, give an overview of the structure of the key message that you will be delivering.
CHANGE SIGNALS	Indicate clearly when you are switching topics. For example: "I will now talk about…."
VISUAL/VERBAL HOOKS	Use images, graphs, charts, or spreadsheets to highlight points, and emphasize key words.
HANDOUTS	Prepare copies of the presentation and any relevant supporting material.
PACING	Alter the speed of your presentation to suit the fluency of the audience.
BODY LANGUAGE	Be aware of cultural differences and omit gestures that might be confusing,

THINGS TO DO

1. Consider what thoughts you want to leave your audience with.
2. Brainstorm ideas on content, flow, and methods.
3. Identify your key messages and adapt them to suit your audience.
4. Rehearse the presentation several times beforehand.

ADAPTING PRESENTATIONS

Consensus cultures like a relatively low-key, formal presentation with a lot of background information, visuals, and handouts. The audience will be attentive, but not very participative. Autonomy cultures tend to like short, well-structured, and dynamic presentations with a relatively small amount of context. Supporting data is important. Expect many questions. Status cultures like a warm, personal touch, and a "soft-sell" approach. They are likely to interrupt regularly and want to engage in dialogue. Gently guide them back to the topics you want to discuss. They will appreciate your flexibility.

CONDUCTING NEGOTIATIONS

Negotiating is a critical skill for global managers. To be effective at cross-border negotiation, find ways to work around cultural differences so that the outcome is acceptable to all parties. Use well-tried tactics and be well prepared.

73 Be clear about what you will accept and what you will concede.

POINTS TO REMEMBER

- Most cultures want to feel they are winning a debate.
- In many consensus and status cultures, a written contract will be less important than a handshake. In these cultures, overly legalistic contracts may be perceived as a lack of trust.
- In many parts of Asia, a contract is never final. It is always open to renewed negotiation as circumstances change.

ADAPTING YOUR STYLE

Cultural style influences the pace of negotiations, as well as the strategies, decision-making, and contractual arrangements used. Negotiations in autonomy cultures tend to be fast, but are tied up with legalities. Negotiations in consensus cultures are often slow, and require trust, which is built up over time. Contracts are likely to be broad, and subject to change as circumstances alter. People in status cultures also like to take time to form trusting relationships. They may become impatient with overly legalistic contracts.

CONSIDERING FACTORS

Before a negotiation, ask yourself some questions:
- Why? – List the risks and opportunities for both sides in the negotiations.
- When? – Consider the factors, such as budget cycles or the market, that will influence timing.
- Where? – Think about the advantages and disadvantages of specific locations.
- Who? – Look at the status, age, and gender of those involved. Consider including a third party.
- How? – Judge the amount of time that should be spent on task versus relationship issues.

CULTURAL DIFFERENCES

The Western tendency to be direct can be perceived as confrontational by those in cultures that put great value on relationships and prefer indirect communication. The respectful deference of an Asian can be seen as a weakness by a Westener.

THE NEGOTIATION PROCESS

PREPARATION
Identify objectives, cultural differences, and shared interests

STRATEGY
List questions to ask and determine team roles

OPENING
Introduce yourself and create a positive atmosphere

UNDERSTANDING
Listen more, talk less, and look for common ground

BARGAINING
Emphasize mutual interests and make concessions slowly

CLOSING
Reiterate agreements and follow them up in writing

74 Take a break if you have reached a deadlock.

PREPARING YOURSELF

Make sure that you understand the context of the negotiations that you will be taking part in. Gather fundamental information about the other party and its country of origin. Assess the decision-making style, hierarchy, and underlying interests of the organization. Gauge the economic development, and the monetary, fiscal, and trade policies of the country it is based in, as well as the telecommunications and transportation networks. Understand the country's political ideologies and foreign policies, and make a point of studying the legal tradition and business law. Make sure that you appreciate the values and beliefs, language, and customs of the country too.

NEGOTIATING SKILLS

Keep your language plain and simple and make sure that everyone understands the meaning of what you have said. Minimize surprises, because these will put the other party on the defensive. Focus on all parties' mutual underlying interests. If you see the situation as a problem that you all want to solve, you will avoid getting into a deadlock. Never rush: Patience beats impatience every time. Build trust, and always focus on a win-win result.

Emphasizes key point

► **BEING CLEAR**
Keep reiterating shared interests, even though your opening positions seem far apart.

49

MANAGING CONFLICT ACROSS BORDERS

Working across a variety of cultures increases the chance that there will be misunderstandings and clashes of opposing interests. Accept the challenge and adapt your strategies so that any conflict is constructive, rather than destructive.

75 Think carefully before adopting your usual way of handling conflict.

CULTURAL DIFFERENCES

In Japan, leaders are expected to preserve *wa* (harmony) and to avoid open conflict through co-operation and a caring attitude. In the United States, conflict is expected to emerge naturally when different interests compete.

CULTURES AND CONFLICT

Generally, autonomy cultures expect conflict. Individual interests will often clash with one another and with the organization. The best ideas and people are thought to emerge out of competition. Consensus cultures typically avoid open conflict, although confrontation can occur when there is no risk of damaging the group or of losing face. Although feelings are openly expressed in status cultures, there is a dislike of conflict and aggressive, adversarial styles.

COPING WITH CONFLICT

There are five strategies for managing conflict, ranging from passive to active. Passive strategies include avoiding (keeping the conflict under the surface) or yielding (letting the other party have their way). Active strategies include competing (demanding your way) or creating (collaborating to find a solution). Bargaining to find a compromise is a middle path between active and passive.

USING PERSUASION ▶

This manager is bargaining with a customer. He is appealing to his customer's emotions and relying on their good relationship to help him reach an agreement on a contract.

ADAPTING STRATEGIES

Managers tend to rely on one or two conflict-management strategies. However, when you work globally, you need to be able to use all five. Using only avoiding and yielding will not help you in autonomy cultures, where the emphasis is on competing and creating. Relying on a competitive strategy will not succeed in consensus cultures, where avoidance and indirectness are valued. To gain credibility in status cultures, be ready to compete, but be prepared to bargain, which is often accompanied by emotional appeals to friendship.

76 Adapt your strategy, depending on the context.

77 Avoid mistaking emotion for hostility.

LEARNING FROM CONFLICT

Conflict can be constructive when it results in deeper learning about one another and an improvement in communication. Turn every cross-cultural conflict into a learning experience for everyone involved:

● Make sure that the rules for handling conflict are understood by everyone.
● Do not allow personal attacks.

● Use conflict to bring cultural differences into the open.
● Make sure that you demonstrate your appreciation of these differences.
● Look for ways to highlight shared interests and opinions.
● Encourage open communication and dialogue.

A LEARNING ▶ EXPERIENCE
In this case study, it is the manager's ability to make apologies, even when she did not know what she had done wrong, that allowed the dialogue to move forward in a way that was satisfactory to both parties.

CASE STUDY
Mohammed, an employee in Cairo, called up his manager Linda in New York. After saying hello to him, she immediately asked him what he was calling about. Mohammed, thinking that he had disturbed her when she was busy, tried to end the call, saying he would phone again another time. Linda realized that she had upset him and apologized. She asked him how she had caused offense. He then admitted that

in his culture it was customary to engage in some talk about personal matters and the family before getting down to business, and that her unintentionally brusque attitude had upset him.

With Mohammed feeling more able to communicate under his own terms, they began the conversation again and it was concluded successfully. Their relationship was stronger as a result of their mutual understanding.

LEADING GLOBAL TEAMS

A well-led global team can produce cohesion in geographically dispersed organizations. Understand the dynamics of teamwork, foster good communication, and lead a high-performing team.

RUNNING GLOBAL TEAMS

To run a successful global team, it is necessary to ensure that it is flexible, responsive, and innovative. Ensure that your team is culturally diverse, and includes members whose business activities span the globe and who work well together.

78 Be very clear about how your global team can work together.

▲ **USING TECHNOLOGY**
When your team members work in different countries, use communication technologies, such as video conferencing, so that staff feel part of a larger team.

WHAT IS A GLOBAL TEAM?

A global team brings together people with the experience, knowledge, and skills to fulfill an organization's goals. For example, strategic global teams identify or implement initiatives that put the business in a better position in the marketplace. Operational teams focus on the efficient and effective running of the business across the whole network. They include information technology teams and head office teams.

79 Be very positive about your team's capabilities.

80 Make every team member feel valued.

EXAMINING ROLES

Culturally diverse global teams perform three valuable roles. First, they create a global view of the business, while having a sound knowledge of local realities. Second, they have the potential for generating creative ideas and making fully-informed decisions. Third, teams representative of the organization's international base are in a better position to ensure that new procedures are implemented throughout the business. Understand that no one person has all the answers in a global environment, and develop a "collective" intelligence.

ASSESSING DYNAMICS

Global teams can produce exceptional results, but they can also be dysfunctional. Dysfunction can be caused by many factors: if there are too many people of one nationality, they may dictate to the rest; language difficulties can result in the exclusion of one or more people; over-politeness may mean people repress real views. Recognize these issues and work to counteract them.

81 Make sure that your team is able to share ideas and information effectively.

EXAMINING THE FUNCTIONS OF GLOBAL TEAMS

Team members who are based in various locations around the world can bring together specialized knowledge and insights. Together, they can produce a unique and valuable overview of the global market. Their roles may include:

- Analysis of external and internal risks to the business.
- Alertness to new opportunities, such as possible new markets to enter.
- Coordination of global projects, activities, and processes.

- Development of global strategy, products, services, and training.
- Responsiveness to new trends in the market, such as increased competition.
- Experimentation to generate radically new ideas and to test them.
- Integration of business activities to create efficient interaction.
- Transference of technologies, best practices, and knowledge.
- Assessment of diverse customer needs in key markets.

DEALING WITH TEAM EXPECTATIONS

Cultural background shapes expectations about the role of a team. It also affects how members relate to each other and to you as team leader. Integrate the team and make sure that you satisfy the requirements of each individual team member.

82 Recognize your own cultural expectations of teamwork.

83 Look at how teamwork styles might complement each other.

ALIGNING THE TEAM ▼
A leader needs to understand the different perspectives of team members and work toward building common understandings.

FOCUSING ON TASKS

Teamwork in autonomy cultures is task-centered and the team has specific objectives. Members are often individual specialists with particular roles and responsibilities. Meetings tend to have clear agendas and produce tangible results. Spend time on tangential issues, but guide the discussion back to the agenda. Recognize that tension lies between the pursuit of results and the need to provide the rewards, such as recognition, expected by individual members.

Team leader
guides discussion

Sales executive wants
consensus on decision

Publicity director feels everyone
should be responsible for their
own decisions

WORKING AS A COMMUNITY

In consensus teams, results are achieved via well-ordered relationships. Total team agreement is the intended outcome after thorough deliberation of all the perspectives. Competition within the team is not expected, but strong rivalry between teams is typical. Bear in mind that much of the contentious work could be done outside of meetings. Use meetings to exchange information or affirm decisions already made. Make use of group protocols and well-defined agendas.

THINGS TO DO

1. Encourage members on global teams to talk about past team experiences.
2. Find out what worked for them and what did not.
3. Ask them how they would like this team to operate.

WORKING AS A CLAN

Because of the need to maintain differences in rank, teamwork in status cultures can be difficult. An autocratic/paternalistic leader will control all decisions, while other members simply express opinions. Loyalty, personal allegiances, and obligations play significant roles in what is done, how, and by when. Be aware that the team's purpose is often defined over time, and agendas will be relatively free-flowing. Although outcomes may be unpredictable, remember that a successful meeting will reinforce team relationships.

84 Balance tasks with building relationships.

85 Use differences to spark greater levels of creativity.

REINFORCING TEAM RELATIONSHIPS

Your management challenge is to create an inclusive team, with a common vision and mission, in which everyone can contribute their best work. Always aim to allow individuals to maintain their identity. Use expressions like:

We will succeed as a team by allowing our differences to complement one another.

Let's learn from each other the ways we can create better value for our customers.

Whatever our differences, it is important to remember that we share the same goals.

We're in this as a team, and together we can solve any problem that comes our way.

ASSESSING GLOBAL TEAMS

Global teams bring together all the ingredients for success, but also for disaster. Accept that it is your responsibility to help your global team work well together, identify and improve its strengths, and be prepared to tackle its weaknesses.

> **86** Be flexible about how you expect team members to contribute.

VALUING PEOPLE

Successful team players contribute to a team in three ways. First, they recognize cultural differences and are willing to collaborate across them for the advantage of the organization. Second, they have the necessary strategic expertise and market experience. Third, they have the requisite communication and interpersonal skills.

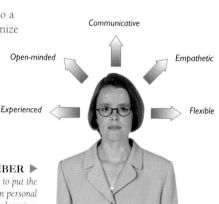

Communicative

Open-minded

Empathetic

Experienced

Flexible

A GOOD TEAM MEMBER ▶
Look for people who will be prepared to put the interests of the team above their own personal interests, and who will stay open to learning.

> **87** Create a database of good global team players.

> **88** Give your global team direction and purpose.

FOCUSING ON A PURPOSE

A strong sense of purpose helps bring together a culturally diverse team because it provides the necessary elements of cohesion and direction. Make sure that everyone on your team agrees about the words used to describe this purpose, and that they understand its meaning. Form a team purpose that consists of two parts: an engaging vision and a clear mission. Vision provides the overall sense of what the team is about. Mission consists of the specific goals and objectives that will enable the team to achieve the vision.

Gaining Participation

Everyone on the team needs to contribute to the work and the final outcome. Create suitable conditions for this to happen, taking into account language and any other cultural differences. Remember that cultural background will shape how individuals on the team like to participate. For example, Americans are comfortable with brainstorming, but many Asians find this practice akin to not thinking about what you are saying. They would prefer to think through their ideas carefully before presenting them. Be capable of enabling different styles of participating to coexist and complement one another.

Fostering Partnerships

In successful partnering, the team generates more than the sum of its parts. Cultural differences can ignite vital energy within a team, producing a "hot" group that performs above expectations. Poor partnering decreases energy, because differences create fragmentation and disorder.

Analyzing the Attitudes of Different Teams

Type of Team	Attitude	Outcome
POSITIVE TEAM	Team members value cultural differences.	Trust
	Team recognizes their interdependence.	Collaboration
	They interact in an honest, respectful way.	Mutual support
	They share views and and are open to learning.	Innovative ideas
NEGATIVE TEAM	Members see cultural differences as liabilities.	Mistrust
	They value their interests instead of the team's.	Unhealthy rivalry
	They interact in a suspicious or defensive way.	Blame
	They keep information to themselves.	My way or no way

DEVELOPING GLOBAL TEAMS

Teams – global or domestic – typically develop through a series of phases, the sequence of which may be affected by change, for example, a member joining or leaving. Recognize what phase your team is in and guide your members forward.

89 Promote team differences as assets, rather than liabilities.

90 Accept conflict among your team as a path to understanding and deeper learning.

FORMING TEAMS

Prepare yourself for team leadership. Be clear about team objectives and learn about each individual. During the first meetings, focus on relationships before tasks. Help everyone relate to each other as individuals. There may be an initial honeymoon period, when differences are treated as interesting novelties – be prepared for this to end. Keep checking for understanding about vision, mission, roles, and responsibilities.

DEVELOPING TEAMS

As work starts, team members will experience the impact of cultural diversity. Make sure that they all understand that differences are expected and welcomed. Express support for variations in expectations about leadership, communication, and so on. When differences emerge, use them to learn about each other and as resources for creativity. If stereotyping emerges when things get stressful, challenge it. Recognize that conflict is expressed and handled differently across cultures. Give time for differing views to be debated. Otherwise, all you will achieve is superficial agreement rather than learning and commitment.

QUESTIONS TO ASK YOURSELF

Q Am I demonstrating an appreciation of the differences on my team?

Q Am I being empathetic to the difficulties others might be experiencing?

Q Am I enabling everyone to participate fully?

Q Am I coaching team members to collaborate effectively?

Q Have I allowed for differences in language fluency and comprehension?

WORKING AS A TEAM

As team members develop shared working practices, ensure that you encourage common ground, but allow for exceptions. Avoid voting on procedures because voting creates majorities and minorities, and builds resentment. Put in writing any agreements that are reached and use these as a reference point. This is useful for reviewing what has been learned, and for sharing it with other teams.

▼ SHARING WITH OTHERS
Create a collaborative team spirit by listening, sharing your knowledge and expertise, and by being open to all ideas.

Team leader guides input of team

POINTS TO REMEMBER

- Encourage competition between ideas, not among team members.
- Celebrate successes, because this will generate strong group feelings and commitment.
- All team members should benefit from any feedback.

91 Be a role model for openness – you will find that your team will be frank with you in return.

PERFORMING AS A TEAM

When the team has achieved its expected potential, it should then aim for even higher performance levels. As the leader, monitor and communicate results to your team. This will help to build pride in team achievements, which will revitalize the team's energy and commitment, especially if it meets infrequently. Work to keep everyone involved and motivated to the end of the project. Make sure that any new members are socialized quickly in the shared methods and culture of the team.

BEING PATIENT ▼
This case study reveals why patience is an asset in a global team. Without it, the whole team can make the wrong decisions.

CASE STUDY

Juan from Spain was on a predominantly native English-speaking team. His English was adequate, but not fluent. The team had been put together to test launch a new product in southern Europe.

During the brainstorming sessions, Juan attempted to communicate his ideas but the others got impatient and kept interrupting him. The native English speakers wanted to put a launch plan together quickly.

By the end of the meeting, a plan had been established, but Juan looked frustrated and confused. He tried to speak to the team leader, but was brushed off, "Sorry Juan, I have another meeting."

Two months later, the test launch had been a failure. In a review meeting, one of the members said to Juan, "I now know what you were trying to tell us. We've wasted a lot of time by not listening and by rushing ahead."

LEADING A TEAM

Global teams bring together multiple sets of skills and diverse working methods. Strong and effective leadership is required for such teams to work well. Be ready to adopt different leadership styles for the various phases of team development.

> **92** Reduce your team's feelings of uncertainty, without overdirecting.

COMMUNICATOR
Explain the team's purpose, roles, and responsibilities

FACILITATOR
Create opportunities for deeper team understanding

INTEGRATOR
Support the development of common working ground

CHALLENGER
Proactively seek higher levels of achievement

COMMUNICATING WITH YOUR TEAM

In the team-forming stage, there will be a lot of uncertainty among team members, who may ask lots of questions. Why has the team been formed? Why am I here? What are the expected results, and when must they be achieved? You might not have all the answers, but communicate what you know honestly and directly. Also, encourage team members to find their own answers, otherwise they may become passive. For example, if someone asks why they are on the team, ask them to say why they think they have been chosen.

◄ LEADING ROLES
As the team develops, the team leader must adopt different roles to help it increase its effectiveness. Keep alert to changes in the team's performance, and alter your leadership accordingly.

ACTING AS A FACILITATOR

In the developing phase, help facilitate differences within the team. Rather than demand compliance, help bring differences in perception and style to the surface, where they can be understood better and managed more effectively. Promote better team interaction through open-ended questioning and help members see shared interests and perspectives. Be prepared to offer guidance for finding a joint way forward.

POINTS TO REMEMBER

- The key challenge for the leader is to emphasize the value that differences bring to the team.
- Help new team members by sharing all the information that they need to succeed.
- Ask for ideas from the team before expressing your own, so that you achieve more input.

93 Be prepared to challenge signs of complacency.

94 Help to bring differences to the surface, where they can be faced.

INTEGRATING A TEAM

As the team begins to work together, you, as the leader and integrator, must help it to balance diversity with cohesion. Help the team develop common working ground (shared values and norms) and begin to act as a role model. Be a willing learner, thoughtful listener, and energetic collaborator. As an integrator, try to improvise with new approaches that make the most of cultural differences. For example, you might begin a meeting with American-style brainstorming, and then end the meeting by defining the actions each person has agreed to do – this more systematic approach is favored by Germans.

CHALLENGING THE TEAM

When the team has achieved a level of self-management, you must still ensure that it is kept focused. Help it to respond and adapt to changes in the business environment. Manage unsettling internal alterations, such as members leaving or joining. While solidifying the team's performance, challenge members to reach higher levels of achievement. Consider yourself to be the agent of change, demonstrate pride in your team, and show an eagerness and enthusiasm for breakthroughs and continuous improvements.

95 Act out of choice, rather than out of habit.

Leader sets targets that will motivate his team

BEING INSPIRING ▶
By working for and with his team, this leader inspires members to overcome obstacles and to achieve more.

DEVELOPING A TEAM CULTURE

Global teams need to shape a common culture that provides all members with shared expectations and a sense of belonging together. Recognize that the team culture will evolve over time, but it can be accelerated by getting early agreement on shared values.

96 Balance diverse interests and views with a common team culture.

97 Focus on communicating and listening.

COMMUNICATING WELL

The key to great teamwork is communication. Make sure that you and team members agree to keep language plain and simple. Take time to clarify any assumptions and keep checking for differences in meaning and perception. Ensure that everyone listens to what is being said. As the team leader, keep looking out for nonverbal behavior that indicates confusion or resistance, such as a frown. Encourage others to do the same. Set a pace that is comfortable for the whole team.

SHOWING RESPECT ▼
In this example, when a team member arrives late, the leader reminds her that the team appreciates promptness.

Team member arrives late for meeting

Leader reminds employee about punctuality

Colleague is impatient to start meeting

ENCOURAGING LEADERSHIP

Reaching peak performance requires leadership behavior from everyone. This will involve team members challenging their conventional thought patterns, as well as each other's limiting beliefs about what can be done. Encourage your team to be proactive, and help them deal with any friction before performance is affected. Resist any individuals or subgroups who seek to impose their views, but remember to focus on solving problems, not assigning blame.

98 Respect the values and culture of individual members, but remind them to work as a team.

SHARED VALUES

The leader must ensure a high level of trust on the team. Trust strengthens commitment. Encourage the following values:

- Empathy – have concern for the well-being of all.
- Fairness – treat each other equally, without bias.
- Honesty – relate to each other straightforwardly.
- Respect – value each other's differences and contributions.
- Sharing – share knowledge and expertise to produce the best outcomes for the team.

THINGS TO DO

1. Work with the team to agree on ground rules, such as punctuality or how to handle conflict.
2. Write these rules down and distribute them to all team members.
3. Periodically review the rules at team meetings, and collectively evaluate how well the team is following them.

FOSTERING GOOD ORGANIZATION

Provide a sense of structure in your organization, so that procedures are clear. Encourage your team to define their roles so that everyone knows what is expected of them; record these definitions to avoid misunderstandings. Manage the workflow: make it clear who will receive what from whom and by when. In this way, you will help your team to manage its time and processes so that targets are achieved. Review progress regularly.

▼ **MONITORING PROCESSES**
Make sure that all your team members know their roles, and are aware of schedules and deadlines. Monitor performance, achievements, and results.

| Define roles | Manage time | Review progress |

RUNNING REMOTE TEAMS

Global businesses operate in an increasingly networked world. More and more teams consist of people in multiple locations and time zones. Recognize that the success of your team depends on developing cohesion, communication, and interaction.

99 Keep e-mail communications to the point, but retain pleasantries.

100 Always keep cultural differences in mind.

101 Follow up verbal communication in writing.

MANAGING REMOTELY

Connectivity, confidence, and commitment are critical for the success of remote teams. A strong sense of connectivity unites a team across time and distance. Be a good role model for communication. Use technology but do not neglect the "human touch." Be sure that you and your team members are confident that everyone on the team will fulfill their responsibilities. Without full commitment, morale and goodwill disappear very quickly. Both are difficult to retrieve when members are widely dispersed.

REAPING REWARDS

There are no special formulas for managing globally – all businesses are different and are constantly changing. Work closely with your global customers, partners, and colleagues to create value out of your differences. Stay in touch with all aspects of your organization, from the grass roots up. It is a demanding task, but the rewards of good global relationships are priceless.

KEEPING IN TOUCH ▶
Make sure that you can contact and communicate with your team members, customers, and partners wherever you are in the world.

STRATEGIES FOR RUNNING REMOTE TEAMS

TYPE OF STRATEGY	IMPLEMENTATION
SHRINK THE DISTANCE	Hold some face-to-face meetings and establish regular communications. Set up intranet-based biographies to enable team members to learn about each other. Return phone calls within half a day.
LEVERAGE TECHNOLOGY	Choose a form of communication available to all members and appropriate for the task (e.g. video conferencing so that all the team are involved in a meeting). Follow up telephone calls in writing to ensure agreement on meaning.
SPOTLIGHT CULTURE	Before making a telephone call, remind yourself that the receiver has a different culture, and adjust your communication accordingly. Put a world map on your office wall, highlighting where your team members are located.
COMMUNICATE CONTEXT	Choose the appropriate technology for the context. Video conferencing, for example, reveals body language and voice tone, as well as facts, whereas a fax machine exchanges information only.
ENCOURAGE PARTICIPATION	Avoid feelings of isolation by establishing emotional links, such as celebration of success, between team members. Be fair to everyone, encouraging ideas from all, and never relying more on those who are physically closer to you.
MAINTAIN FOCUS	Create goals and mission statements, role descriptions, task and process charts, schedules, and reviews. Communicate regularly to prevent members being focused on local issues, thereby neglecting the global overview.

ASSESSING YOUR CROSS-CULTURAL SKILLS

Evaluate your readiness for global management by reading the following statements, and then choosing the option that is closest to your experience. If your answer is "never," circle Option 1; if it is "always," circle Option 4, and so on. Be honest with yourself. Add your scores together and refer to the analysis to see how you scored. Use your answers to identify areas that need improvement.

OPTIONS
1 Never
2 Occasionally
3 Frequently
4 Always

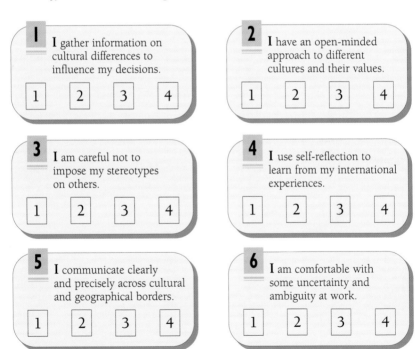

1 I gather information on cultural differences to influence my decisions.

1 2 3 4

2 I have an open-minded approach to different cultures and their values.

1 2 3 4

3 I am careful not to impose my stereotypes on others.

1 2 3 4

4 I use self-reflection to learn from my international experiences.

1 2 3 4

5 I communicate clearly and precisely across cultural and geographical borders.

1 2 3 4

6 I am comfortable with some uncertainty and ambiguity at work.

1 2 3 4

7 I am patient with other people as they learn to adapt their working techniques.

1   2   3   4

8 I look for opportunities to gain valid cross-cultural experiences.

1   2   3   4

9 I make sure everybody working with me takes cultural differences seriously.

1   2   3   4

10 I keep checking for shared understanding in cross-cultural work.

1   2   3   4

11 I adapt easily and effectively to new situations.

1   2   3   4

12 I take the time necessary to build trusting and strong relationships.

1   2   3   4

13 I listen attentively and accurately, giving plenty of time to each speaker.

1   2   3   4

14 I make sure that everyone in my team feels included.

1   2   3   4

15 I can empathize with other people so that they know they can rely on me.

1   2   3   4

16 I can recognize my own biases and work toward managing them.

1   2   3   4

17 I anticipate the effect of cultural differences on business issues.

| 1 | 2 | 3 | 4 |

18 I always try to integrate opposites into mutually beneficial solutions.

| 1 | 2 | 3 | 4 |

19 I make sure my staff members attend cross-cultural training sessions.

| 1 | 2 | 3 | 4 |

20 I pay attention to my global management development needs.

| 1 | 2 | 3 | 4 |

21 I create opportunities to talk about cultural differences with my team.

| 1 | 2 | 3 | 4 |

22 I seek and use feedback on my global management performance.

| 1 | 2 | 3 | 4 |

23 I try to create the right conditions for everyone to do their best work.

| 1 | 2 | 3 | 4 |

24 I pay attention to the value cultural differences can add to the business.

| 1 | 2 | 3 | 4 |

25 I try to understand the cultural orientation of our business associates.

| 1 | 2 | 3 | 4 |

26 I resist judging people if I do not understand their culture and circumstances.

| 1 | 2 | 3 | 4 |

ASSESSING YOUR CROSS-CULTURAL SKILLS

27 I make sure that I show respect to others who are different from me.

1 | 2 | 3 | 4

28 I am eager to share my international experiences with others.

1 | 2 | 3 | 4

29 I nurture a sense of humor to support relationship building.

1 | 2 | 3 | 4

30 I am confident in my ability to manage in different cultural contexts.

1 | 2 | 3 | 4

31 I make sure everyone understands the organization's ethical values.

1 | 2 | 3 | 4

32 I use cross-cultural conflict to deepen our learning about each other.

1 | 2 | 3 | 4

ANALYSIS

Now that you have completed the self-assessment, add up your total score and check your performance. Whatever level of success you have achieved, there is always room for improvement. Identify your weakest areas, and then reread relevant sections to establish and hone your global management skills.

32-64: As yet, your global management skills are limited. Set goals for yourself so that you can improve your effectiveness.

65-95: You have a good grasp of many global management issues, but you need to develop your skills to be wholly effective.

96-128: You are a skilled global manager, but remember that the international marketplace is always changing. Stay focused on continually improving your knowledge and skills.

INDEX

ACKNOWLEDGMENTS

AUTHOR'S ACKNOWLEDGMENTS

It was a delight working with skilled professionals like Kate Hayward and Laura Watson at Studio Cactus. Many thanks go to Adèle Hayward at Dorling Kindersley for the opportunity and encouragement. Great thanks to Laurie Quinn for turning pencil scribbles into wonderful graphics. Thanks also to my colleagues at Transnational Management Associates for their support – Christopher Crosby, Hans van der Linden, Stephen Pritchard, Russell Harlow, Mark Brodermann, Jody Schubert, and Sheeba Mulbocus.

PUBLISHER'S ACKNOWLEDGMENTS

Dorling Kindersley would like to thank the following for their help and participation:

Editorial Amy Corzine; **Indexer** Hilary Bird; **Photography** Gary Ombler.

Models Roger André, Philip Argent, Clare Borg, Angela Cameron, Kuo Kang Chen, Russell Cosh, Patrick Dobbs, Kate Hayward, Richard Hill, Janey Madlani, Maggie Mant, Brian Monaghan, Karen Murray, Frankie Myers, Kerry O'Sullivan, Lynne Staff, Suki Tan, Wendy Yun **Makeup** Nicky Clarke.

Picture researcher Samantha Nunn; **Picture librarian** Melanie Simmonds, Hayley Smith.

PICTURE CREDITS

The publisher would like to thank the following for their kind permission to reproduce their photographs:

Key: t=top, b=bottom, r=right, l=left, c=center
Corbis: Ronnen Eshel 4c
The Image Bank: Derek Berwin 21tr; Flip Chalfont 17tr
Image State: AGE Fotostock 9tr, 64br
Corbis Stock Market: Jon Feingersh 52bl; Jose Luis Pelaez Inc 6bl
gettyone stone: Arthur Tilley 19tl

Jacket photography © Dorling Kindersly and Eyewire
All other images © Dorling Kindersley
For further information see: www.dkimages.com

AUTHOR BIOGRAPHY

Terence Brake is a leading authority in global management consulting. He is President of Transnational Management Associates (tma) – USA, working closely with clients such as Arthur Andersen, Hewlett Packard, and Vivendi Universal. He has facilitated numerous global business workshops in Europe, Asia, and the Americas. His books include *Doing Business Internationally* and *The Global Leader.* In 1994, he was awarded the American Society for Training and Development's International Professional Practice Area Research Award. His personal mission is to help make cross-cultural understanding part of mainstream life in the United States and beyond. He may be contacted via email on tbrake@tmaworld.com